* Sarah Doret *

WHAT HAPPENED IS HAPPENING

SARAH
DUET

Copyright © 2022 by Sarah Duet

All rights reserved.

To request sharing permissions, contact sarah@sarahduet.com.

ISBN (Paperback): 978-0-57837-161-0
ISBN (E-book): 978-0-578-38533-4

First paperback edition: March 2022

Cover art, images, and interior design by Sarah Duet
"FLORIA" © 2021 by Sarah Duet (Cover painting)

Printed in the United States of America

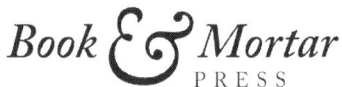

Book & Mortar Press
Shreveport, LA

*For survivors of the COVID-19 pandemic
& in memory of every life lost*

CONTENTS

Introduction

I.	CHAOS	15
II.	CARE	31
III.	HISTORIES	55
IV.	BREATH	75
V.	IMAGINATION	103
VI.	MYSTERY	121
VII.	CHOICE	147

Source Texts
Acknowledgements
How to Make Blackout Poems
About the Author

INTRODUCTION

What Happened is Happening is a collection of blackout poems that I made during the COVID-19 pandemic. The process of erasure I used to compose them emerged as a welcome release valve for the compounding thoughts, feelings, and questions arising within me during this turbulent time.

In mid-2020, I felt bottlenecked creatively. There was so much to say, to contemplate, to process, to ask. Yet it was difficult to get any of it out. My previous methods and mediums were failing in the current context. So I turned to this new-to-me technique and was surprised to find a much-needed creative flow.

In retrospect, this shouldn't be surprising. I have learned over time that it is often easier to create what I like to call *something from something*. The expanse of the blank page can be paralyzing with all its possibility, and sometimes it helps to kickstart one's creative energy by remixing what already exists. Whether that's through collage in visual art or erasure in poetry, it is astounding what newness can arise and how much one can communicate with seemingly so little material.

How does it work? After "blacking out" most of the words on a page of found text—from newspapers, old books, or magazines—what remains creates new meaning in the form of a poem. The result is a visual art piece as much as a literary one. Some say the poems resemble redacted FBI files, while others see tiny constellations written in the night sky of the page. The method highlights the significance of what is *not* said as much as what is.

This process has been a lifeline for me, and I've been heartened to see how many of these poems resonate with you, the readers, as I share them. It is the encouragement of those connections that moved me to compile this printed collection.

—

You know the cliche: Hindsight is 20/20. We can see more clearly with additional information, looking back to better understand our experience. And in many ways, the year 2020 offered us a rare opportunity for hindsight. It revealed truths about our individual and collective experiences that many of us had previously been able to avoid seeing—whether through distraction, denial, or privilege. The virus that caused this pandemic may have been novel, but the vulnerabilities it has exposed largely are not. So many of the challenges we now face were already present, have only been exacerbated, and can no longer be denied.

The unsustainable pace of a society optimized for efficiency at all costs, increasing inequity, systemic racism, the escalating climate crisis, weakened institutions, rampant individualism, authoritarian fear-mongering, lack of empathic imagination, and our general inability to tolerate uncertainty or solitude are on full display at the collective level. The forced pause—for those with the privilege to take it—made just enough space to turn our attention to these challenges and to examine what they tell us about ourselves. Yes, this has been overwhelming, but we can only change things if we face them and don't look away in a frenzied attempt to return to "normal." Normal wasn't working for many people anyway. In fact, the accepted norms are what put us at risk for the personal, national, and global crises we find ourselves in today.

> "A system built to maximize efficiency is not one that's built to weather disruptions—small or large."
>
> Meghna Chakrabarti,
> *On Point*

On a more hopeful note, we have also seen with greater clarity the human capacities for resilience and generosity and the power of collective action in the face of tragedy. Truly, the only way out is through, as 12-step wisdom teaches us. And if enough of us join our efforts, I believe we can find a better way to move forward together.

At a personal level, I was able to look at my own history without the pressure to maintain such a frenetic pace of life. I identified just how much of life up to this point has been exhausting for me. Many of the changes that the pandemic necessitated—like working exclusively from home, maintaining fewer social obligations, and traveling less—have actually significantly reduced my stress levels and improved my health. Of course plenty of new stressors about viral loads, risk mitigation, missing friends and family, and general existential dread surfaced. But once the dust settled a bit, I could see that so much of what I assumed was required in life was actually optional. Like many people, I'm in the process of reconsidering how I spend my time, the kinds of work I do, and what I do and don't want to bring with me when we finally emerge from this pandemic season.

Between the collective and the personal lies the relational: our connection with friends, partners, family, coworkers, etc. The effect of the pandemic on these relationships, like everything else, is wide-ranging. Ruptures, repairs, stagnations, revivals, and everything in between seem to abound. Some people are thriving while many are fighting to survive, and still others have not made it. Beyond a call for reimagining who we are to each other and remembering that ultimately—whatever a current relationship status suggests—we are not alone, I have little more to say. I don't know what's ahead, but I do know we are inherently connected. What I do affects you; what you do affects me. And we continue to destroy ourselves if we deny that reality. We belong to one another because we exist together in this world—however fraught it may be.

—

What we are seeing is nothing new. What happened in 2020 was already happening. What happened is still happening, and in an all too literal sense. As I write this in January of 2022, the pandemic rages on, our democratic republic is teetering, our healthcare and education systems verge on collapse, and individuals and families are rightfully exhausted. What else could we be at this point?

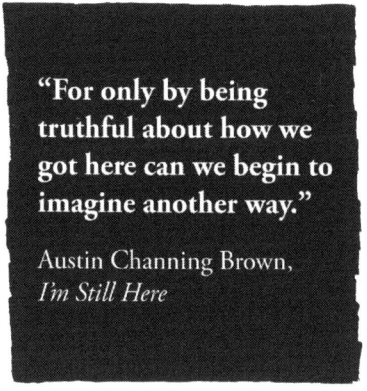

> "For only by being truthful about how we got here can we begin to imagine another way."
>
> Austin Channing Brown, *I'm Still Here*

We would do well to look closely at how we got here. The only way we can create the possibility of a more just, humane, and viable future for us all is to take an honest look at our past and let it shape how we decide to live together in the present. This sort of reflection has to start in the hearts, minds, and bodies of each of us. I hope this small collection of poems might provide a place for some of us to do that work.

I am as ready as anyone for the suffering of these pandemic times to end. I only hope that we don't foolishly leap into the "after" without careful consideration of what brought us here and has kept us here for so long. Truly, what happened is happening. And it will keep happening unless enough of us decide to interrupt it with a better way.

I. CHAOS

Every so often,

Things   heat up

                    a series of
violent catastrophes
                    disasters,
                        like every-
thing else
                        that people
endure, like bad weather.

there is little sense   in
            anything

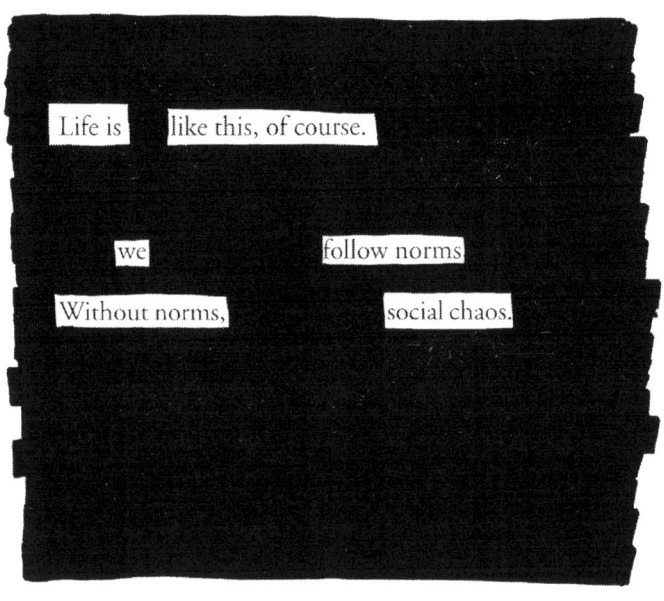

both true and false, fell under suspicion
it was possible to use
errors in a defence

Corona we opened our laptops searching for information God; Google.

more complicated and less hopeful

We couldn't even imagine a day nine months later.

People around the world were praying

the intersection of an ordinary day, his stomach his heart and panic

the reality
For example,
resulted in
relatively uneventful   months afterward
Even now,   I am driving down this same road

We are in uncharted territory

Forget about in-person interaction

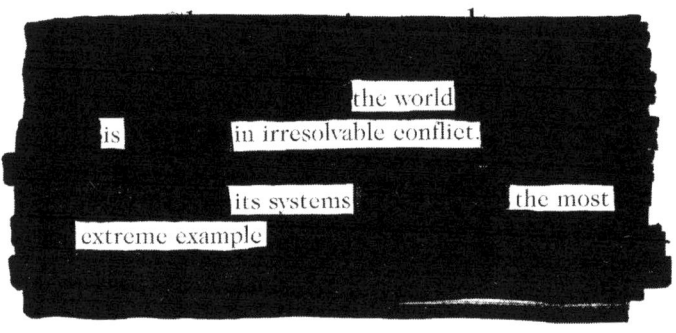

the world is in irresolvable conflict. its systems the most extreme example

What has really happened?

the most callous experiment

With heartless disregard for human life,

just "to see what would happen."

local businesses, along with friends and family on a leash this year. To help fight disease and to improve health Each day, Americans die the killer claims lives every hour

No one can assume

the situation
is
a cosmic regularity
hurry and
argument
industrialized
difference

differences within as well as those between

down-to-earth spirituality
calls for

justice

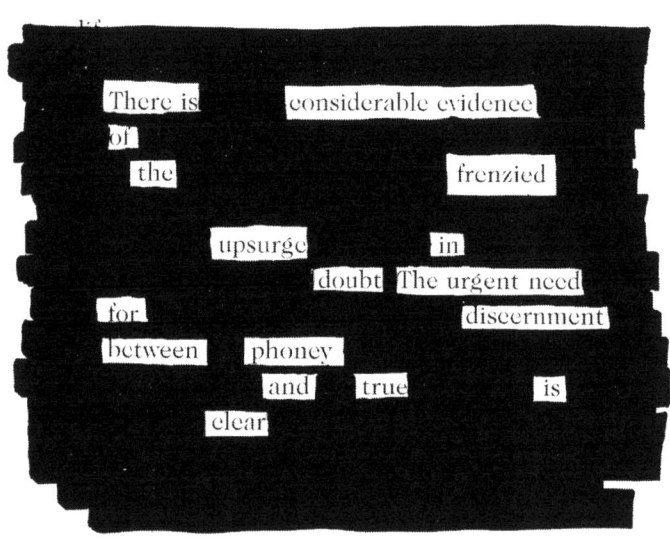

There is considerable evidence of the frenzied upsurge in doubt. The urgent need for discernment between phoney and true is clear

fear
and
the
whole business   of
  manipulating   facts
 disguised refusal

          to believe

expert opinion   as

                          good

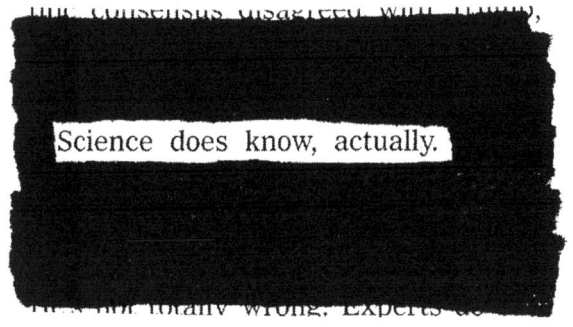

II. CARE

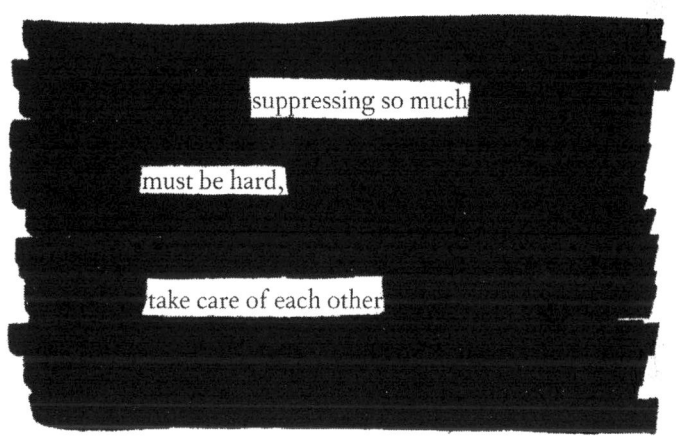

suppressing so much must be hard, take care of each other

people can live with complexity unknown and unknowable.

stop forcing narratives. life doesn't bend perfectly to what you believe

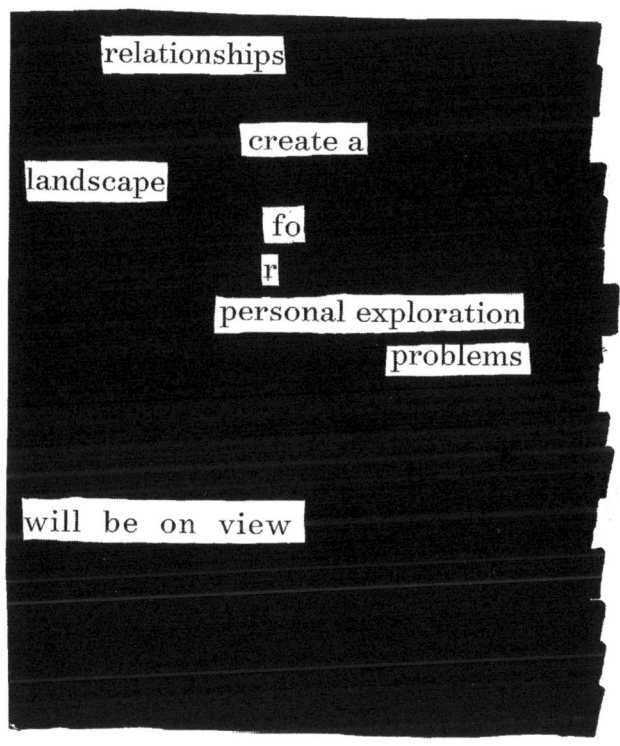

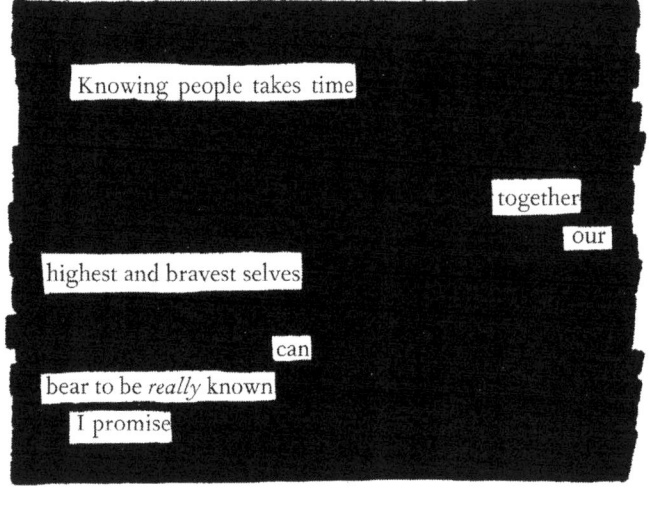

Knowing people takes time

together
our

highest and bravest selves

can

bear to be *really* known
I promise

inclusion makes visible the rationale for a common destination while offering everyone a chance

raise the floor for everybody —
a rising tide lifts all boats

nurture
one
another

take care of the community
we are the community

strength is
connection – here you have a
chance to

ask
questions
rather than just claim
to know–
real, open, and urgent questions. the
work is working together.

conversation

ask smart questions, remember everything and emerge whole

listen

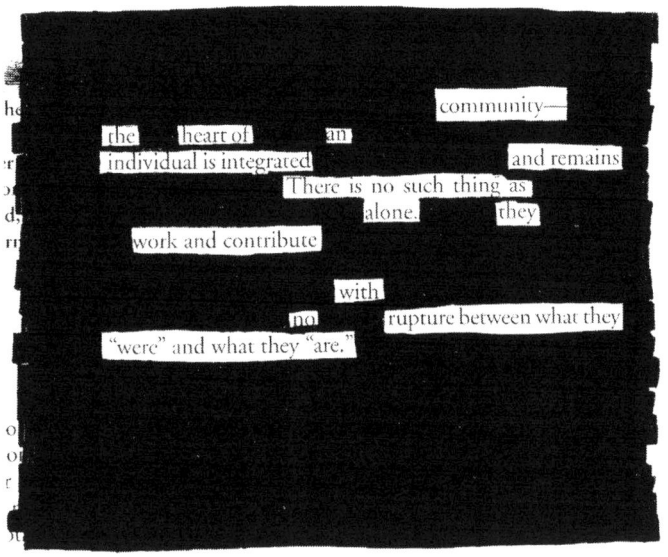

community—
the heart of an
individual is integrated and remains
There is no such thing as
alone. they
work and contribute
with
no rupture between what they
"were" and what they "are."

we interact within expanding networks

extensive connections between individuals everyone eventually included

Think of yourself as part of this

Passion,

On Full Display reveals herself.

Once you free your mind/There is beauty in everything, We're all in this together/ The world needs you now, you matter.

differing and very strong feelings
encounter people

The questions raised
are complex and need answering
with wisdom

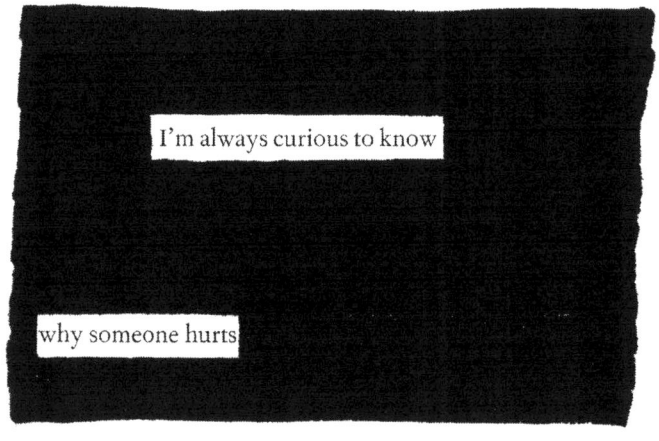

THE INTENTION OF a behavior can reveal much about the pain that provokes it

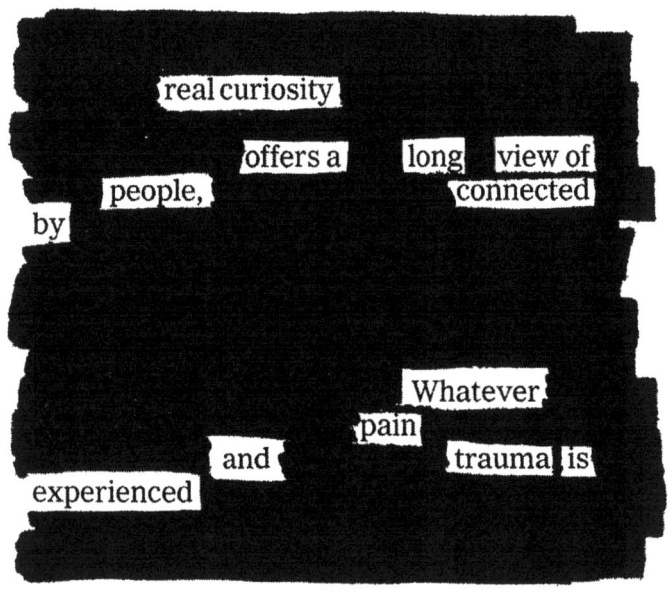

real curiosity
offers a long view of
people, connected
by

Whatever
pain
and trauma is
experienced

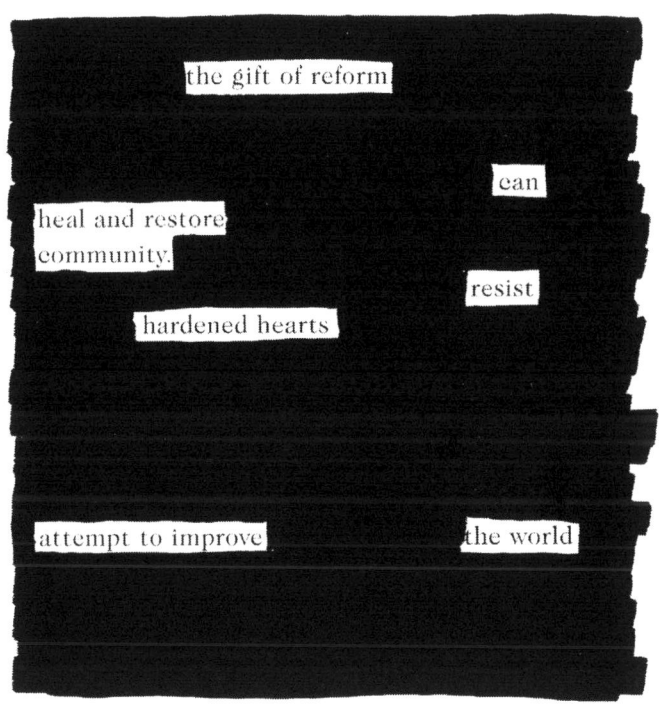

the gift of reform

heal and restore community.

can

resist

hardened hearts

attempt to improve the world

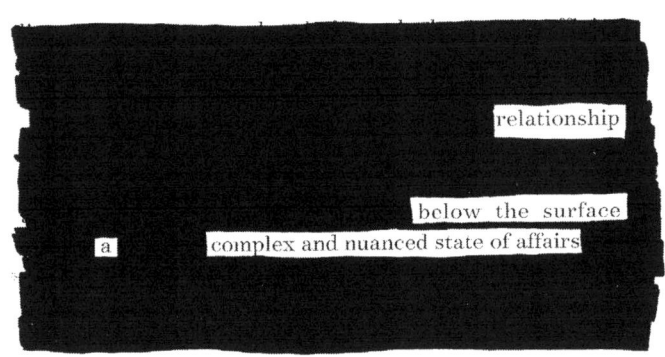

Despite heavy pressure

connections
remained close
all along

before leaving

in spite of every offense and oversight,
we can still
forgive

Our parents,
Our siblings,
Our children,
and Ourselves
for
deficiency—ours, theirs
We love and are loved anyway.

*Thank you for
the love between us.*

We listened

We told stories

We sat at a long table

We took our time
We let ourselves feel
our gratitude

III. HISTORIES

Hidden Histories

you come to realize the stories we know, don't nearly capture our hidden histories. Art unearthed space to reconstruct history and to create an archive of identity uncovering hidden histories.

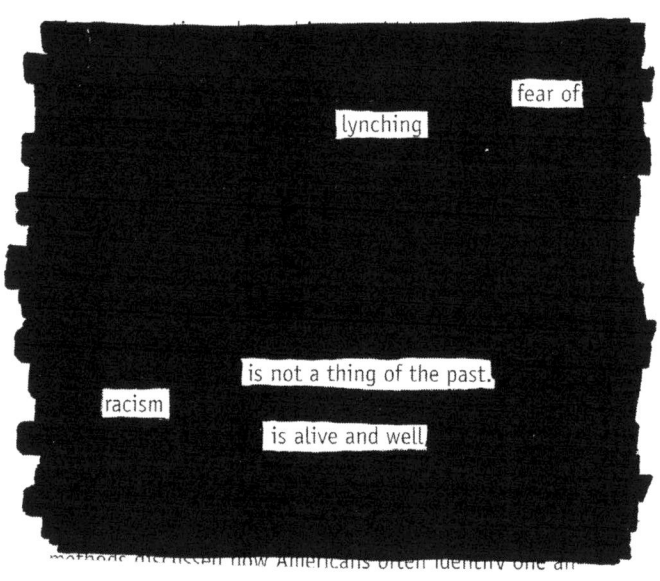

fear of lynching is not a thing of the past. racism is alive and well

this Black teenager
accused
tortured, lynched

his arm stretched out,
is similar to Jesus'

backed by divine law,
But
dismissed by the law of the land

the essence of deep within its soil, that sacred earth.

for generations

Stained scarlet with
the lynchings that took place.
the macabre backdrop
for the struggle to turn towards
the sun again.

living together in difference creates a space to reflect on systematic change, the pause could provide the background, you have to slow down to see the way forward. What equitable future could we write?

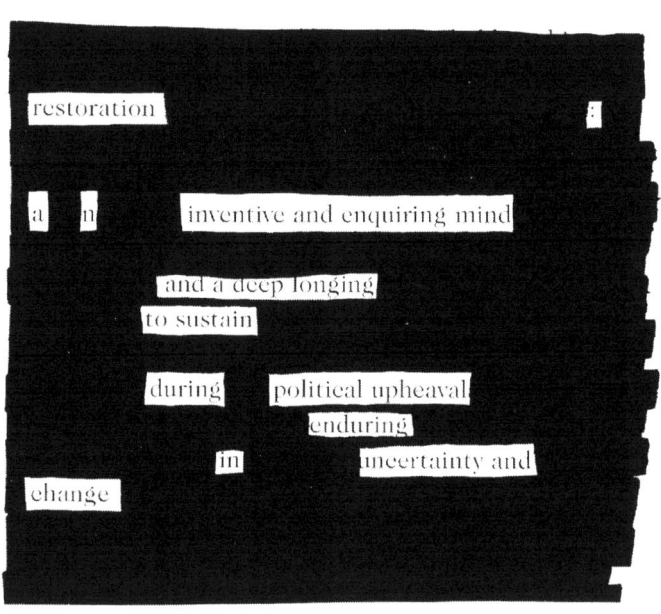

restoration

a n inventive and enquiring mind
and a deep longing
to sustain

during political upheaval
enduring
in uncertainty and
change

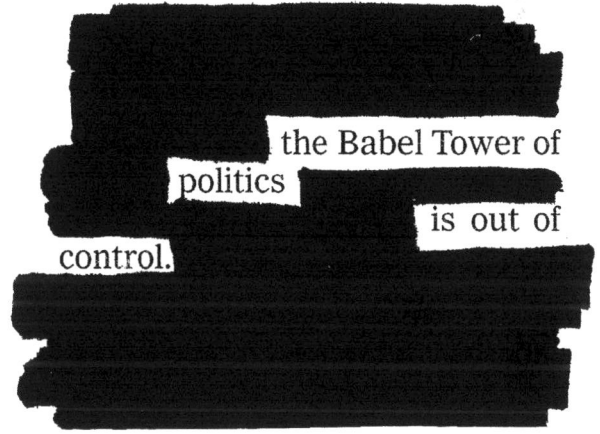

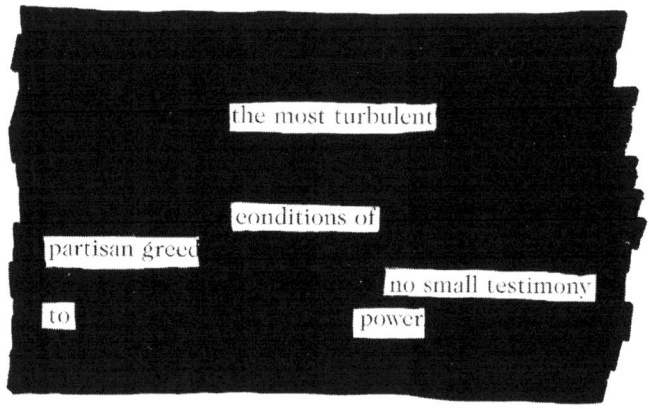

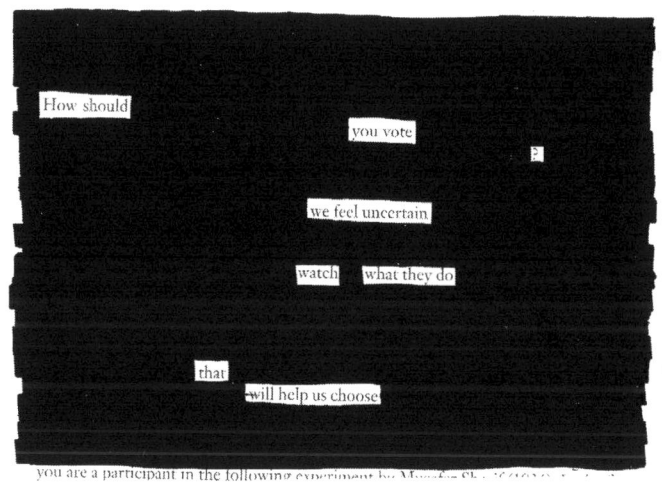

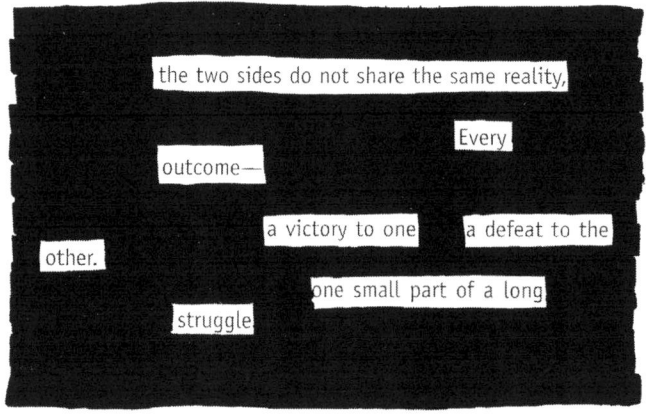

the two sides do not share the same reality, Every outcome— a victory to one a defeat to the other. one small part of a long struggle.

it's a part of American culture. scoring the winning goal ripping her off kneeling on the street

But more importantly,

the lives of ordinary women

make us formidable. who's to tell me I can't persevere through tragedy and loss?

interesting artistic and articulate women can invoke remarkable movements in their lifetimes.

Unhealthful Gaps

Have you heard about

"The gender gap," both a cause and a consequence of unthinking

With the world designed by men being a woman can be a health hazard.

the impact greatest for women of color

the troubling state of our democracy
is sacrificing saints,
administrators are out of touch
an
d oblivious
like

a

dis-
ease
Every conversation fell into the same pattern.

Oh my God, What could he possibly see in a failed government that vandalizes

I would hate
to
magnify

something

so

condescending
I think, rolling my eyes.

Why am I so mad at everyone?

systematically the
disastrous effect
of
being ridden by
untruths   errors and lies
is
consciousness
disown-
ing   its   experience,
there is no truth
what is happening
happen s between one
another

Is this harmful? We don't know. What we have now is the largest uncontrolled experiment in history.

the world will benefit from understanding global challenges. A better future for us all may depend on it.

IV. BREATH

consider

many deep breaths, some counseling.

making pancakes,
walking the dog—

exercise regularly

travel.
read, *work hard but not too hard.*

This is

my fault

No matter what I do

to im-
prove

None of it works

a woman, who listened
said,
You have permission to
stop. That

made room to

look at alternatives.

extreme uncertainty
plays two roles

both tether and propulsion

accelerating us homeward
by God's laws of physics

We must accept that
the plans we made
cannot be carried out

the future is two feelings, loss and hope, simultaneously

Sleep could

fix

every fixable thing.

I understood

with a glass of
water

I

could reasonably hope

Accepting things *as they are* is difficult

Resistance is

suffering on

repeat,

Don't Go to War with
the same thing over and over.

You don't need to be
something you aren't.

the unrelenting stress of
survival mode   feels like

both less and more than

the whole story   take it in.

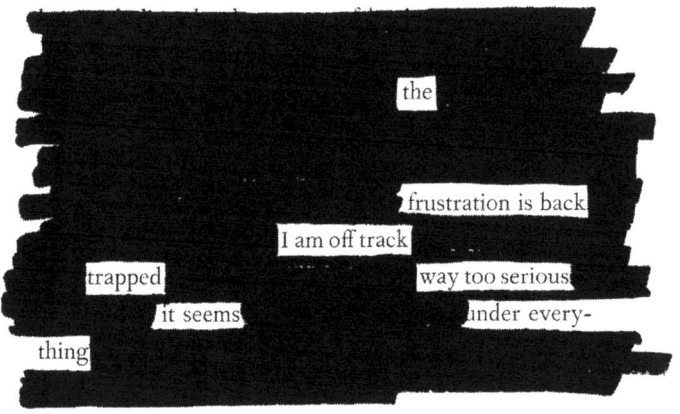

the
frustration is back
I am off track
trapped way too serious
it seems under every-
thing

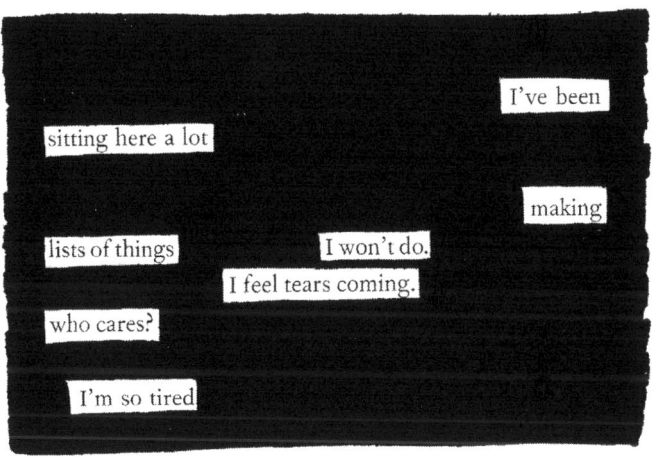

I've been sitting here a lot making lists of things I won't do. I feel tears coming. who cares? I'm so tired

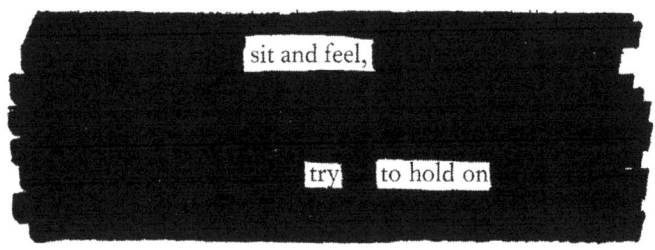

I had so many questions.

At some point, it doesn't matter stop asking and face the grief.

...But

Why did this happen? was all I could think about

H IS FOR HAPPINESS

life isn't a picnic,

death

depression,

plague financial concerns, and soured relationship

face dysfunction with willful optimism.

devise ways out cre-ate a world that is bright and colorful

The demons strive against people who live mainly in their thoughts; warfare conducted on the field of the mind is very difficult to control. Consider this.

The first one was a deeply traumatic matic process My second less dramatic, but still Well-meaning friends said hurtful things "it's for the best," "you're trying too hard." other people Fortunately, understood and allowed me to grieve. I wrote a lot. After about a year I relaxed but I've never forgotten

depression and despair may be fussy, but not frivolous.

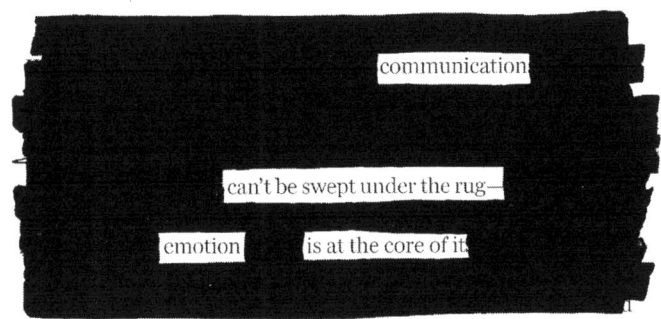

communication

can't be swept under the rug—

emotion   is at the core of it

the Emotion Pump

learn what pleases you and what angers you, use that information to

better encounter "whatever" happens

Think of it as an emotion pump.

you laugh or get angry, the cycle continues.

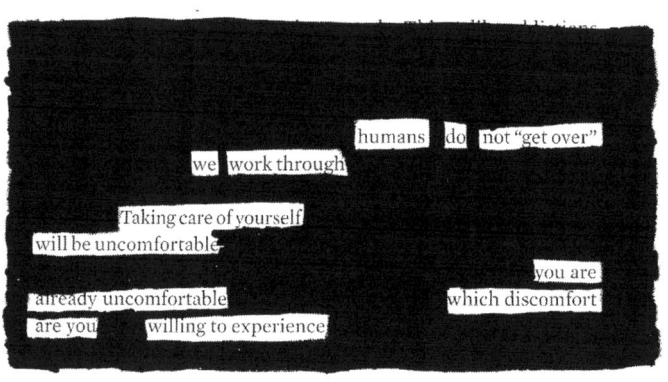

humans do not "get over"
we work through
Taking care of yourself will be uncomfortable
you are already uncomfortable which discomfort are you willing to experience

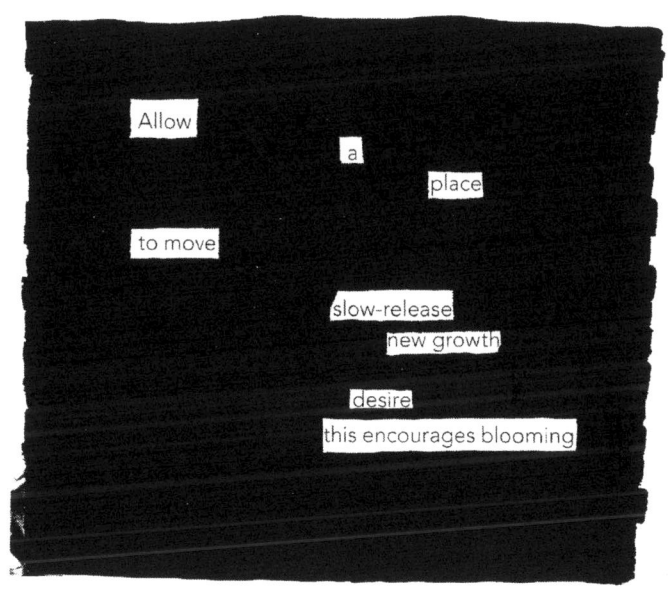

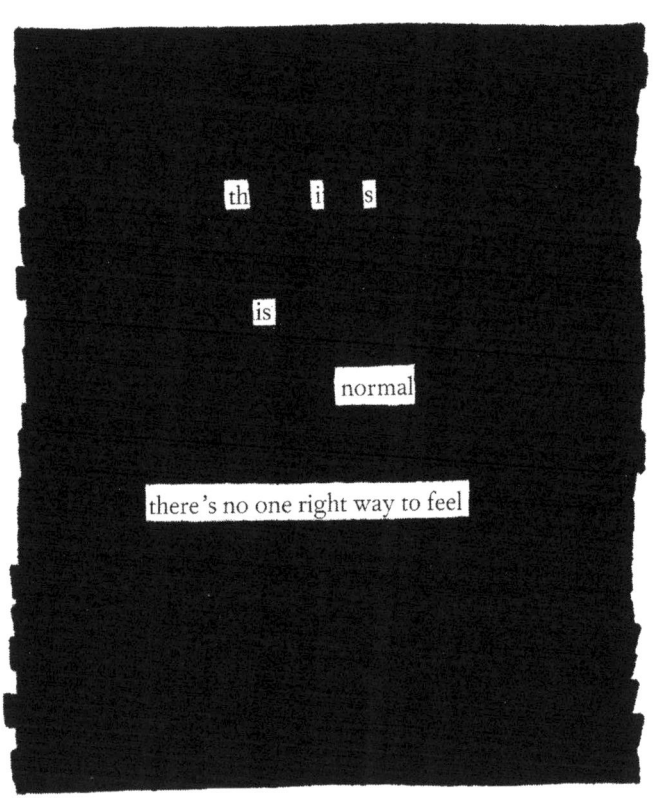

secrets suffocate
the pain of honesty
and integrity
shall 'set you free'.
authenticity

in relationship
fosters

a positive view of
reality.
it helps individuals
reclaim embodiment
and
responsibility in the cosmos.

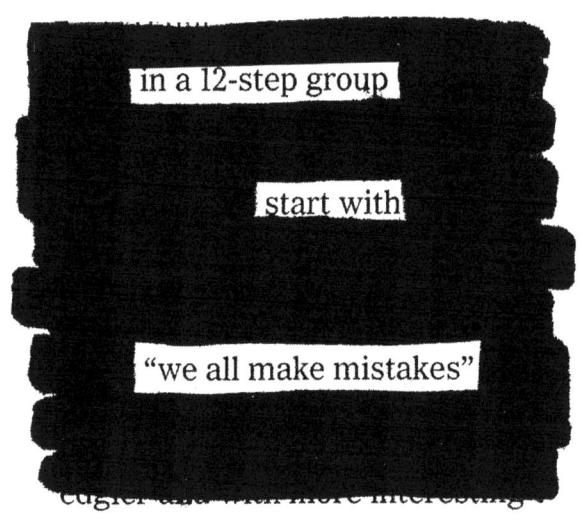

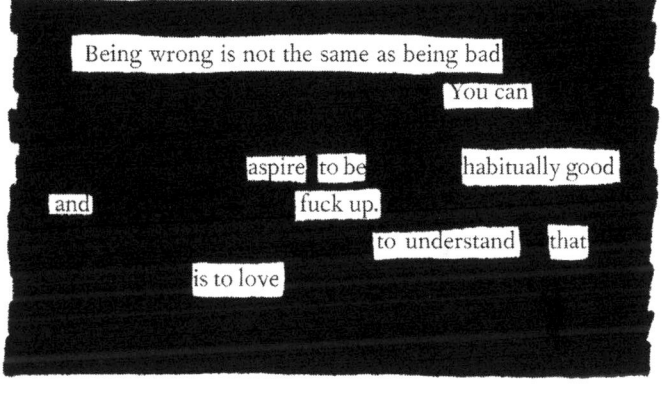

Being wrong is not the same as being bad
You can
aspire to be habitually good
and fuck up.
to understand that
is to love

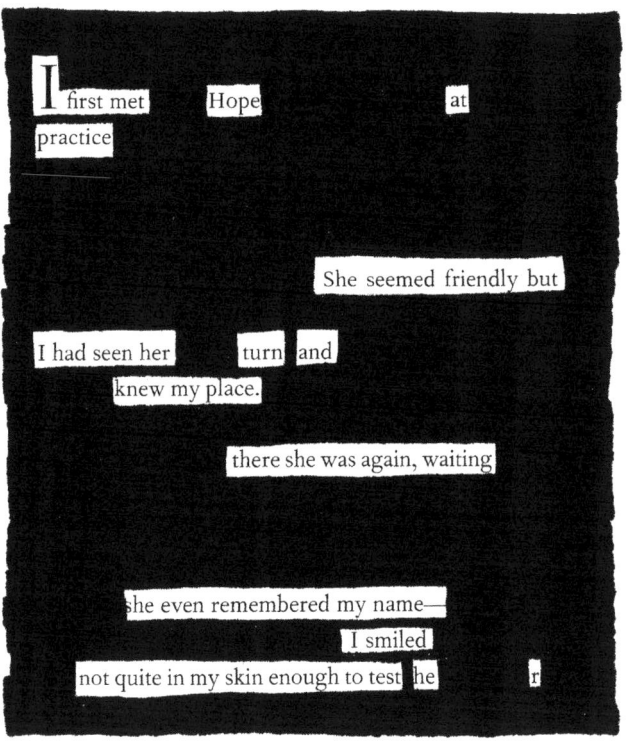

I first met Hope at practice

She seemed friendly but I had seen her turn and knew my place.

there she was again, waiting

she even remembered my name— I smiled not quite in my skin enough to test he r

She's seen it all.

Over dark coffee

She

said thank you a lot.

V. IMAGINATION

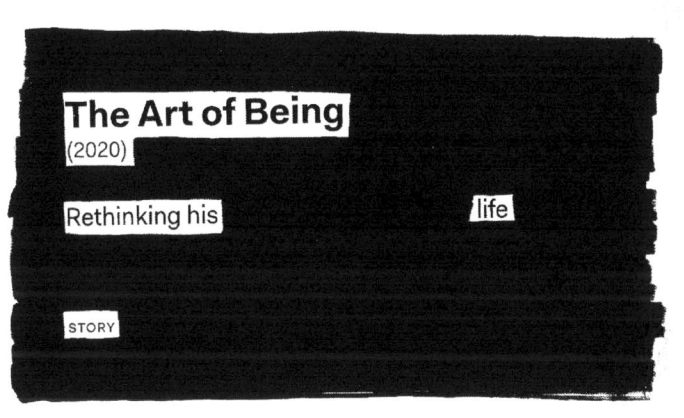

day after day,
persist and explore
in an attempt to
uncover meaning.

create
art using

this process of discovery
and interpretation.

Start with this:

everything

takes a lot of discipline to create

A person

must face this

it's worth learning

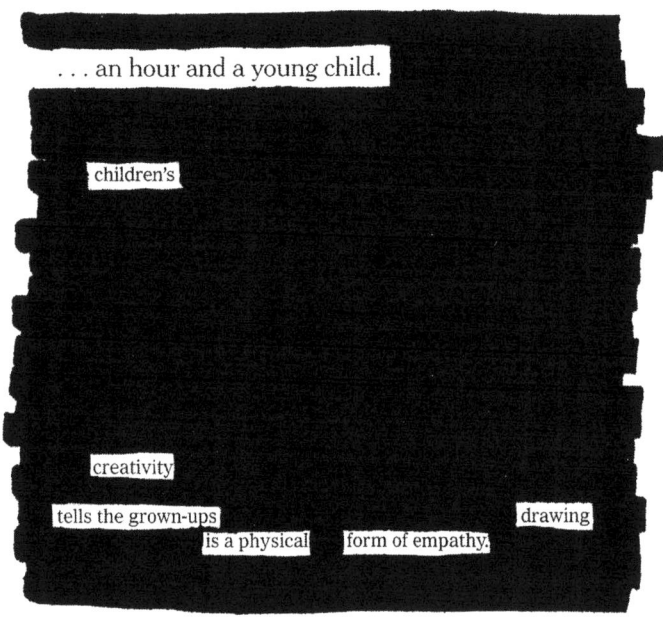

... an hour and a young child. children's creativity tells the grown-ups is a physical form of empathy. drawing

help the kids learn

Now more than ever, to value themselves.

to overcome challenges, and experience adventures where

in "shoulds" don't matter.

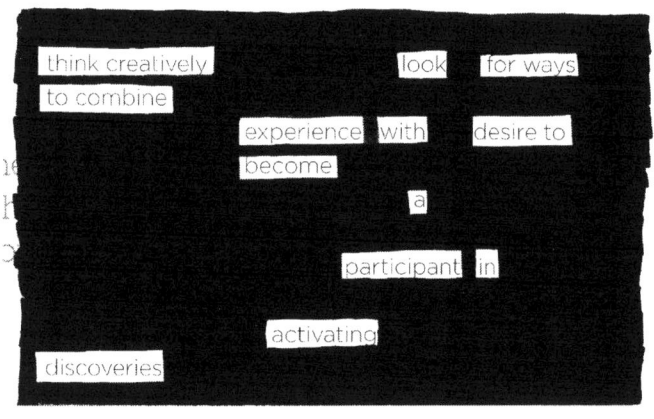

think creatively to combine look for ways experience with desire to become a participant in activating discoveries

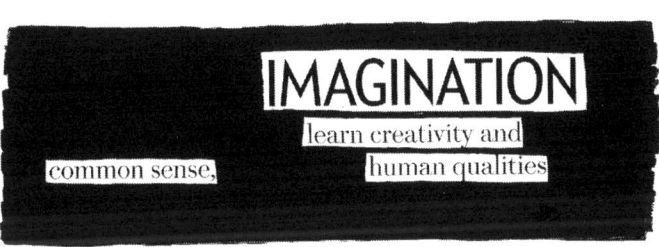

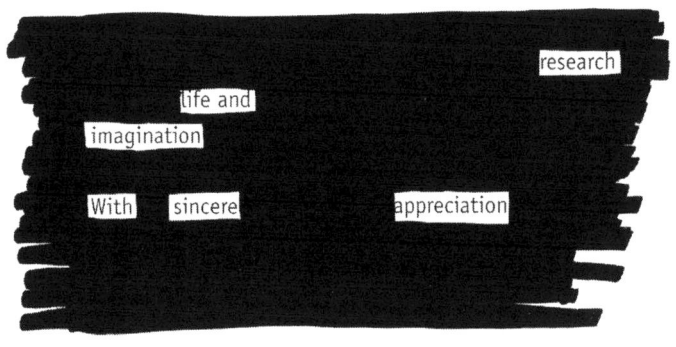

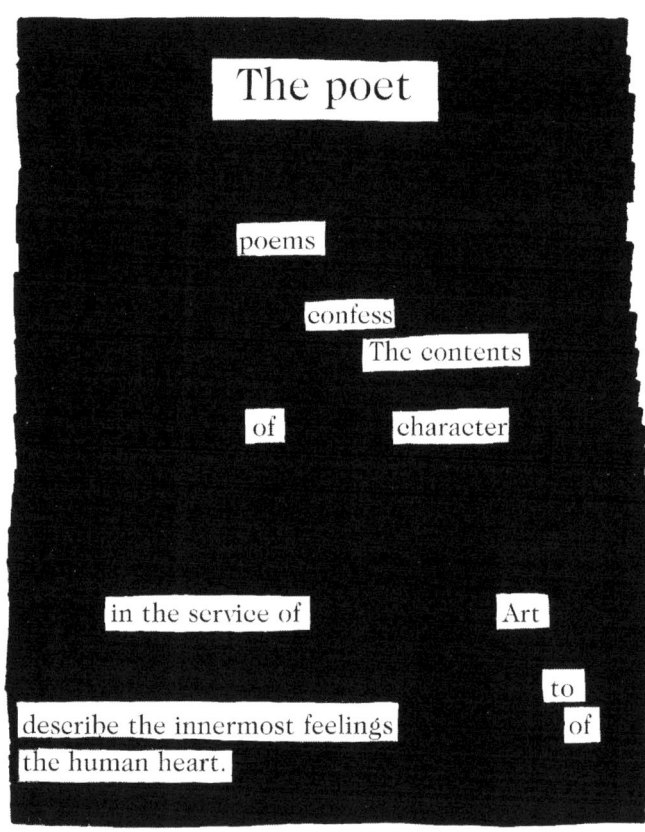

The poet

poems

confess The contents

of character

in the service of Art

to
describe the innermost feelings of
the human heart.

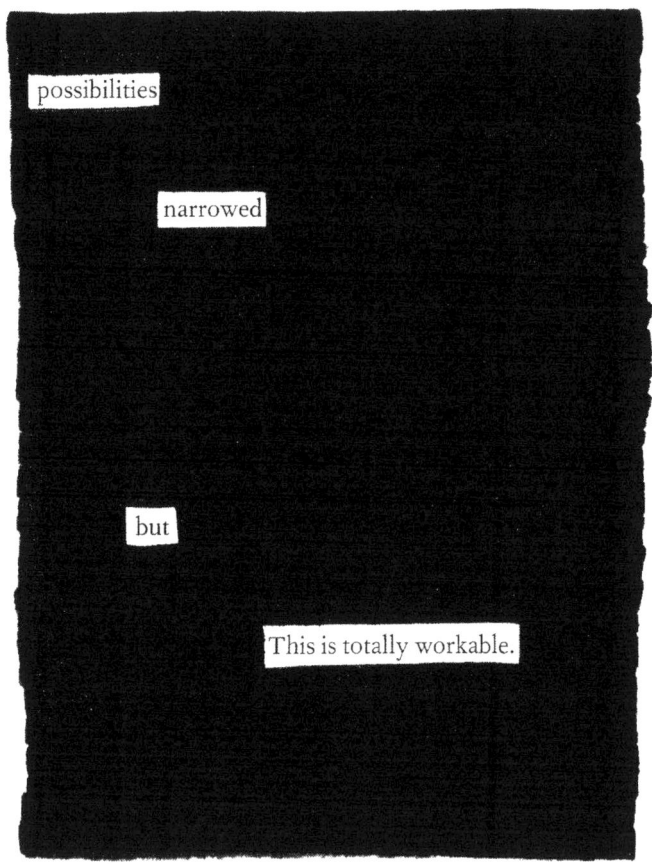

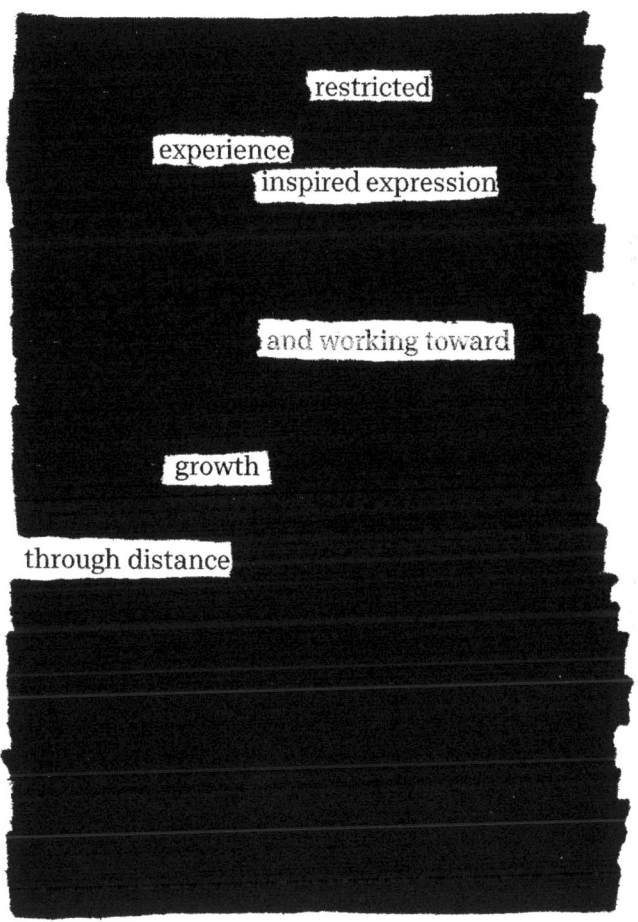

I started to cry,

busy and mad,
had to write,
I slipped away
I locked the door,
and
I vowed to

show up

you get the idea.

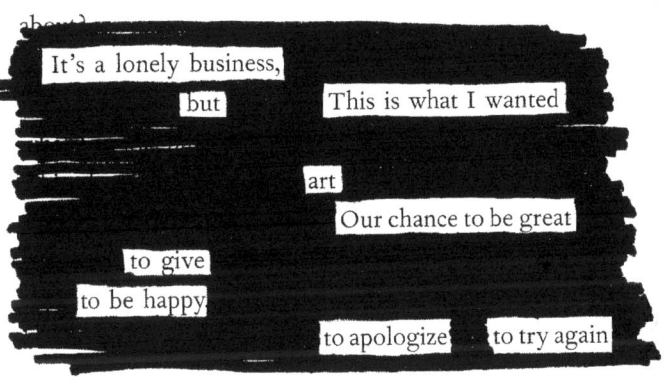

It's a lonely business, but This is what I wanted art Our chance to be great to give to be happy to apologize to try again

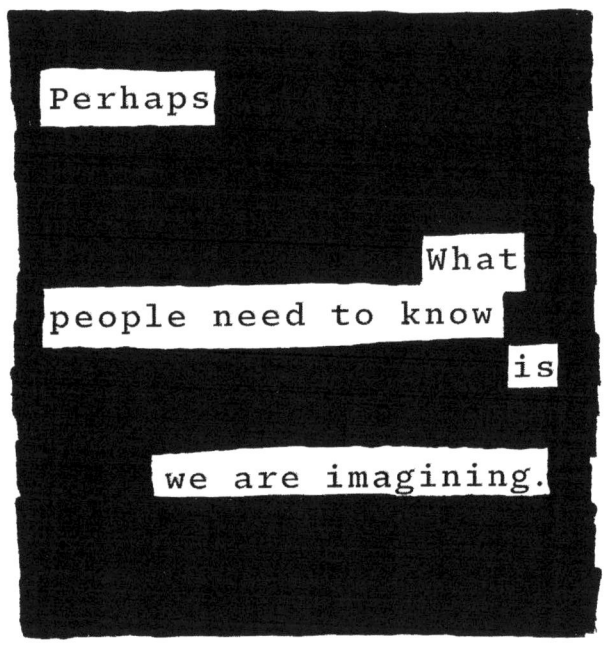

VI. MYSTERY

our wonder
in becoming human

a vital element in

beginning to

create
a generous and
inclusive love

all things are

rooted in the life of the whole

each is dependent on others
our fundamental unity finds expression

'No man is an island'

Holy Commonwealth

'ordinary' saints

serve the

greater

vision

and   nurture lives that

contribute to the   Common

design

of

love

integration: embracing life, every aspect of *desire*, an insistent longing to experience the whole of creation transformed. The two together give vitality and inventiveness, to see life as an *adventure*

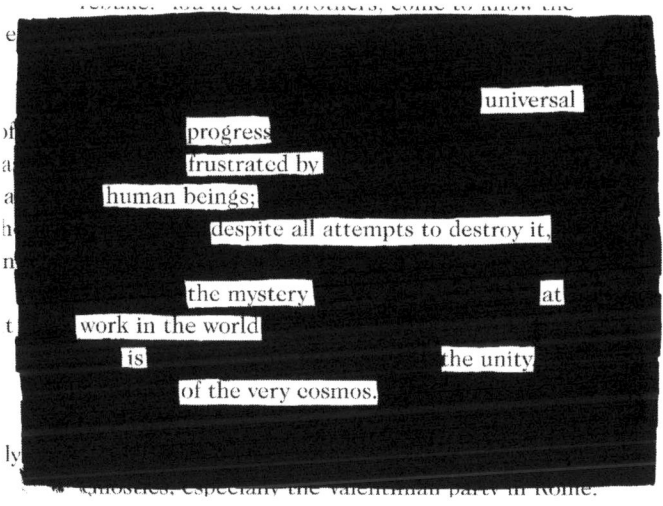

universal
progress
frustrated by
human beings;
despite all attempts to destroy it,

the mystery   at
work in the world
is   the unity
of the very cosmos.

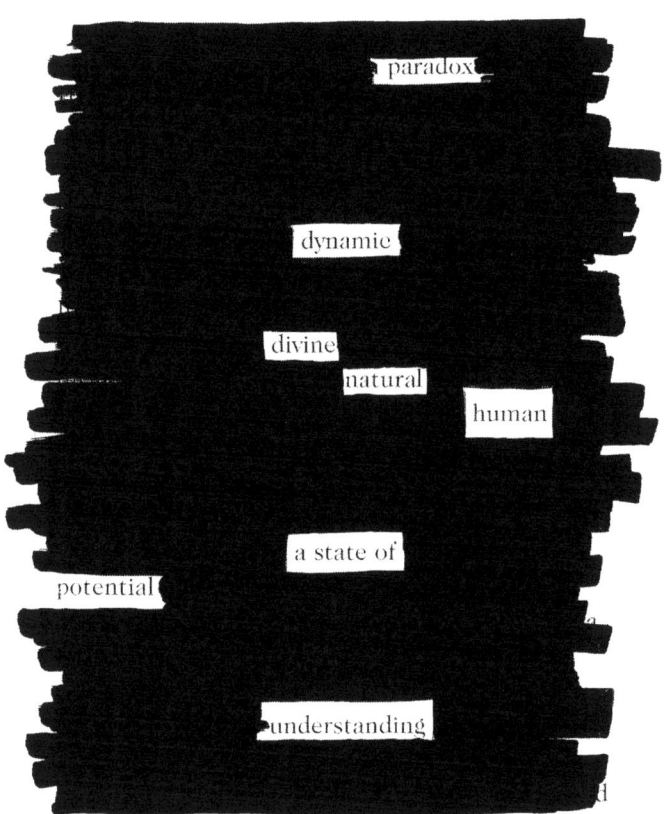

paradox

dynamic

divine
    natural
        human

a state of
potential

understanding

in this
ritual
both strange and
mystical,
I imagine

Wishing others well

communion lets others know

that

anyone
who hears
should
keep going they're not
alone.

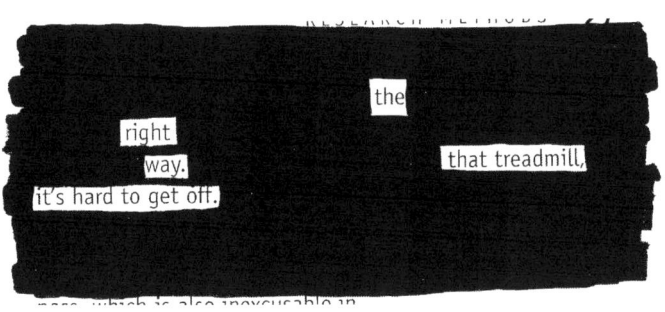

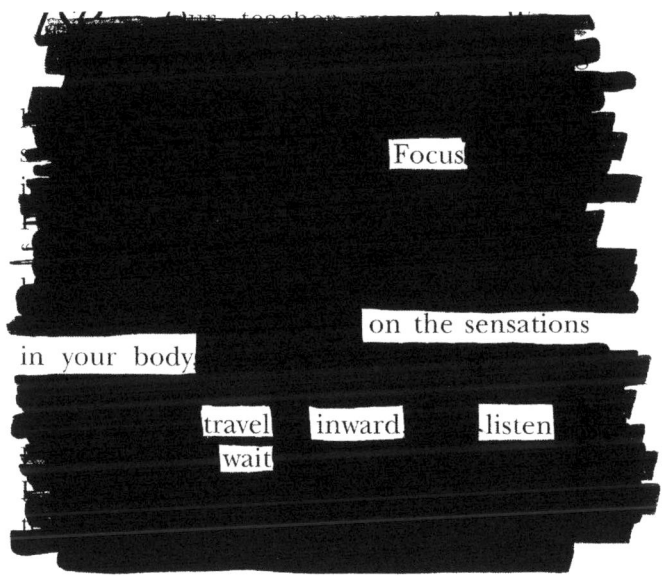

Focus on the sensations in your body.
travel inward listen wait

suffused with
wonder at the beauty of creation

how could I conceivably

seek to possess it?

From Dust I rise,

*A Gift from
The Earth, the Seas,
the Skies*

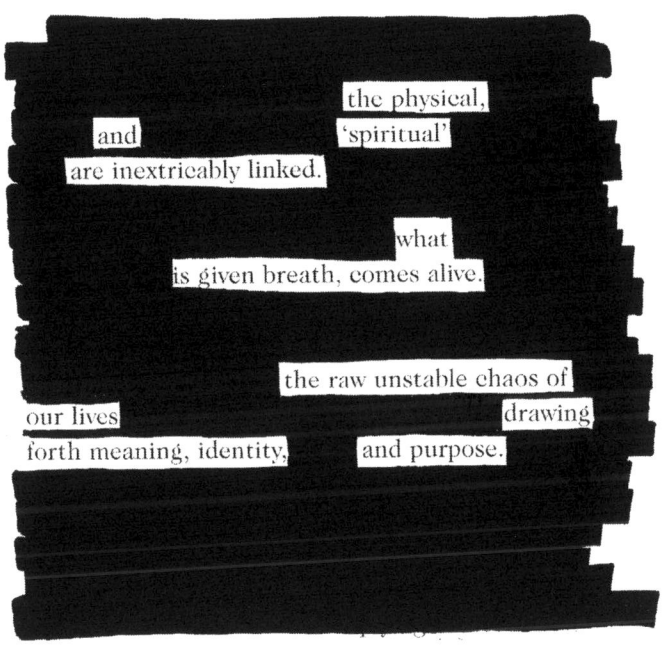

the physical,
and 'spiritual'
are inextricably linked.

what
is given breath, comes alive.

the raw unstable chaos of
our lives   drawing
forth meaning, identity,   and purpose.

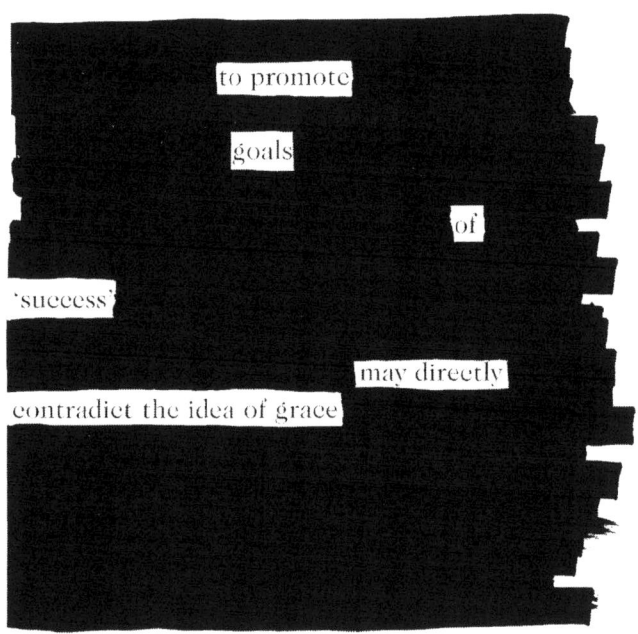

to promote goals of 'success' may directly contradict the idea of grace

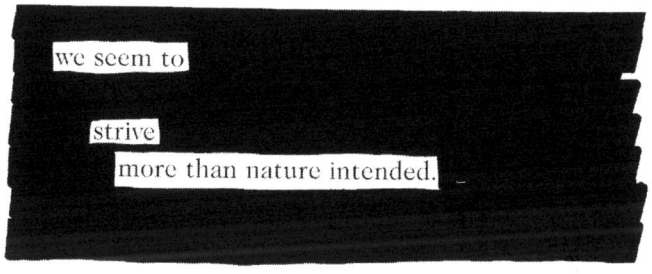

we seem to

strive
more than nature intended.

the ambiguities and sorrows
of human life

challenge

reason,

and
gradually

e   a   n

help   to recover
     spiritual
                    wis
                 d om

I have not known myself

through the
prayers of old men.

all that matters in life is

presence

and

the

desire
to search

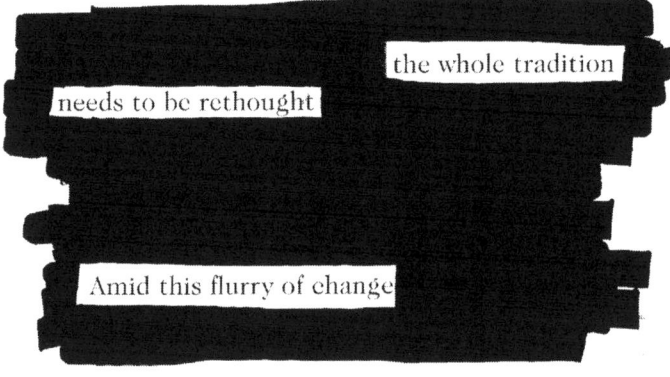

needs to be rethought the whole tradition

Amid this flurry of change

There are questions On the matter of God,

I don't know

I do know
love and gratitude
I wonder I see
and feel But I'm not sure I don't *know*

outside the circle

I
sang our   song,

wanting to find a way back in.
the
need   to
grieve
like cold bathwater

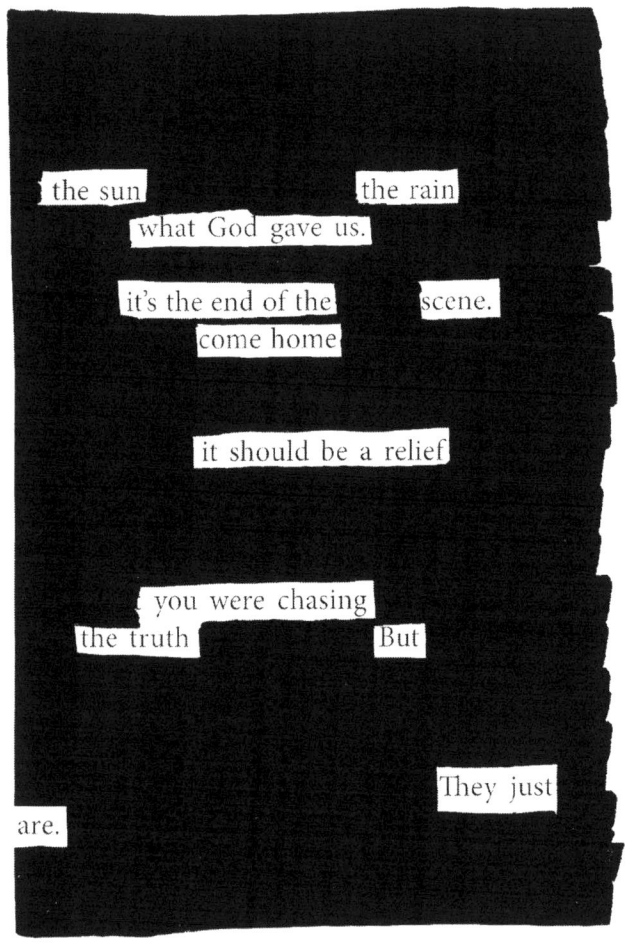

the sun   the rain
what God gave us.
it's the end of the   scene.
come home

it should be a relief

you were chasing
the truth   But

They just
are.

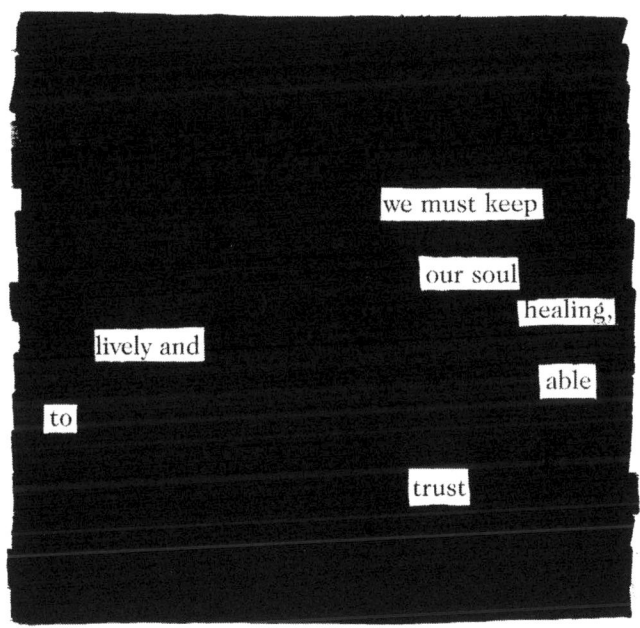

Faith is not constraint. trust only the goodness in life and work actively to revive society.

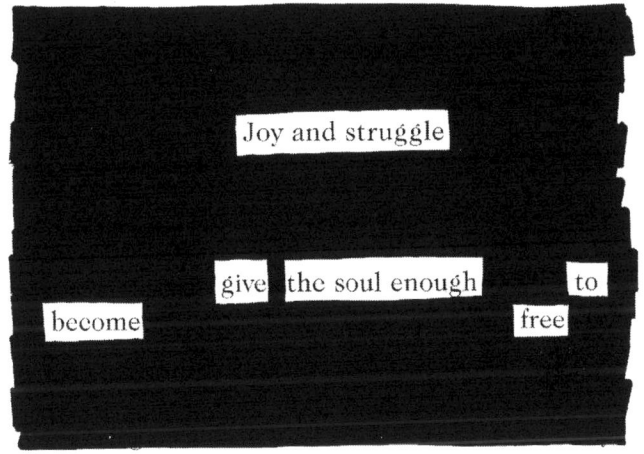

Joy and struggle give the soul enough to become free

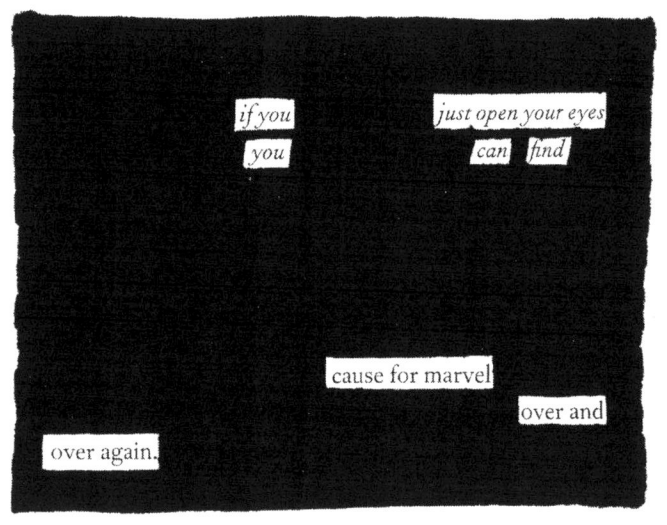

if you   just open your eyes
you   can find

cause for marvel
over and
over again.

VII. CHOICE

Little by little,

you know

what
might have been
rest for a while,
tears

baptize every

de-
tour

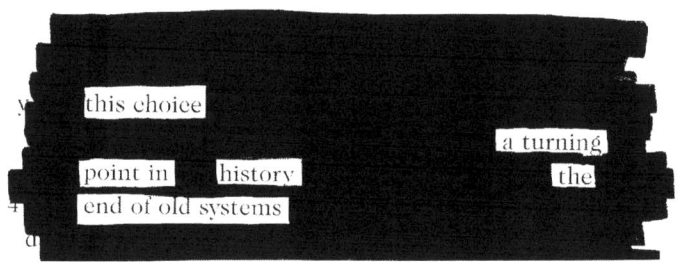

You start to think about where you were supposed to be you didn't want to make a mistake. release regret. *the body knows.*

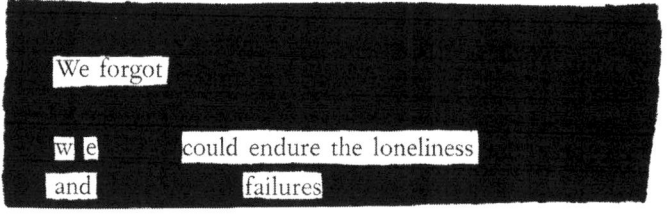

we are recovering from trauma in isolation

Sometimes I miss

vacationing together
planning activities
happy hours

group dinners and
Cleaning dishes after,

We'd discuss
work and
books
and
the stuff of love and anguish

inquiries
Interspersed with
flashbacks

become

engrossing

real and impressionistic
often more
important, than what's

passing
by

The onslaught of unhappiness?
Isolation, despair? crying is

a

Personal Responsibility.

get it out.

And
Do it again.

Go on

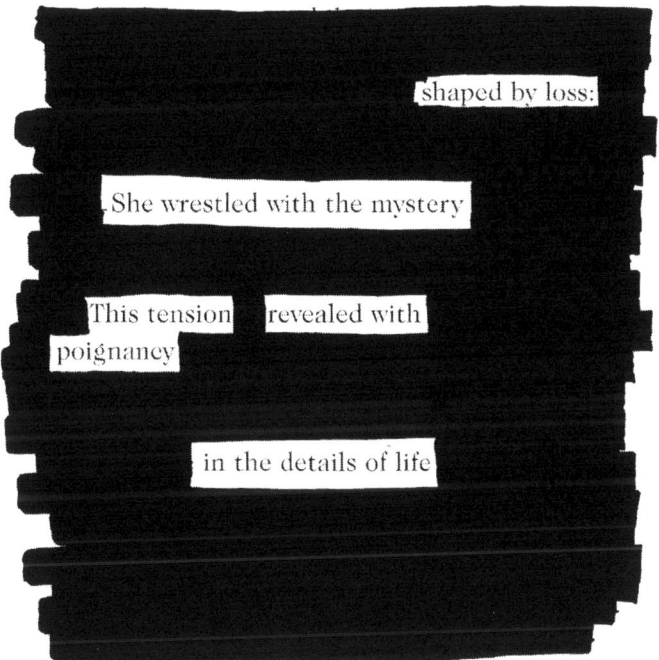

shaped by loss:

She wrestled with the mystery

This tension revealed with poignancy

in the details of life

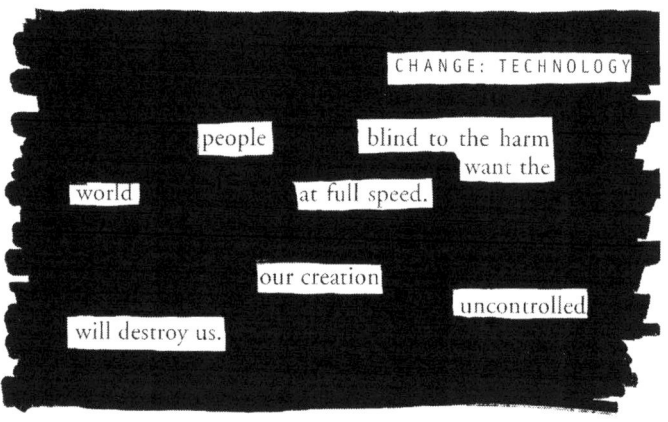

CHANGE: TECHNOLOGY

people blind to the harm
          want the
world   at full speed.

our creation
           uncontrolled.
will destroy us.

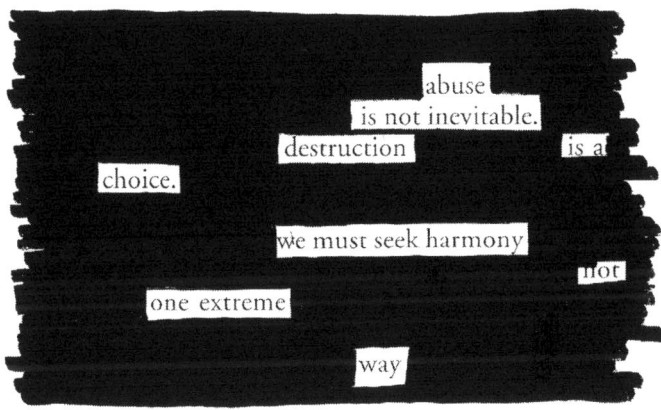

abuse
is not inevitable.
destruction is a
choice.

we must seek harmony
not
one extreme
way

my hope is and compassion will make the world better empathy

This dream is taking shape that will offer resources the challenged, will offer a chance of revitalization of creating a Sanctuary people have embraced new ideas and concepts steadily evolving creating opportunity to move forward authoring a new system, celebrating as they see people thrive

But What Can You Do?

This is a fair question — what can you do

Almost anything! — I was surprised at the answer:

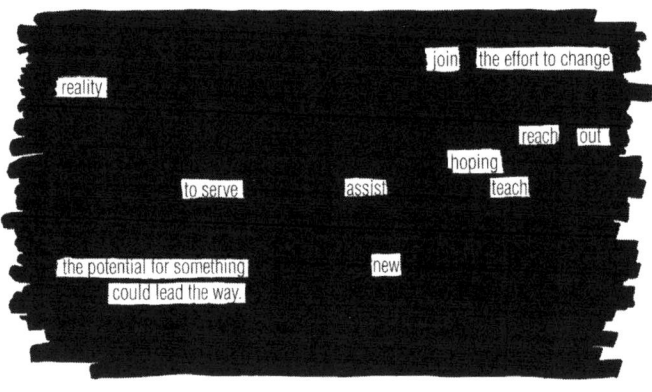

reality join the effort to change
reach out
to serve assist hoping teach
the potential for something new
could lead the way.

uncertainties face the with hope refuse to separate head from heart, individual from community

explore

thoughtful, integrated, rooted

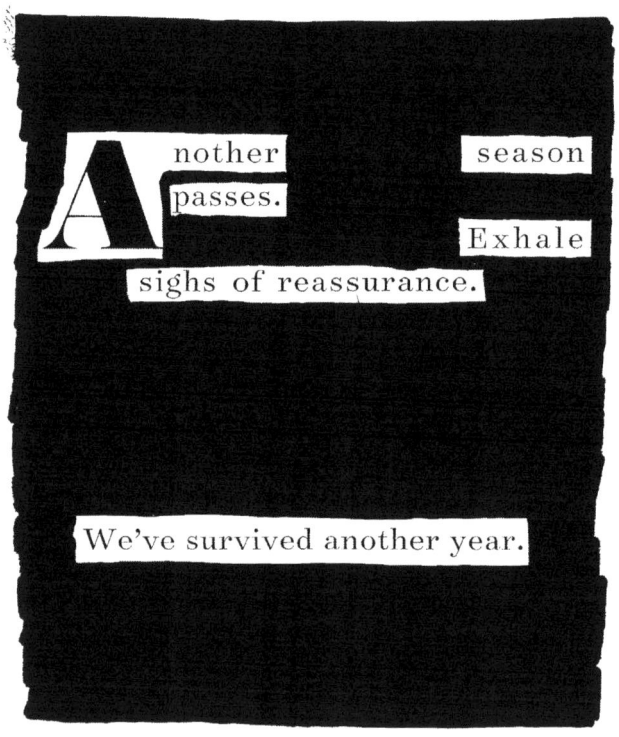

Another season passes. Exhale sighs of reassurance.

We've survived another year.

growth at the beginning near the end, is even greater.

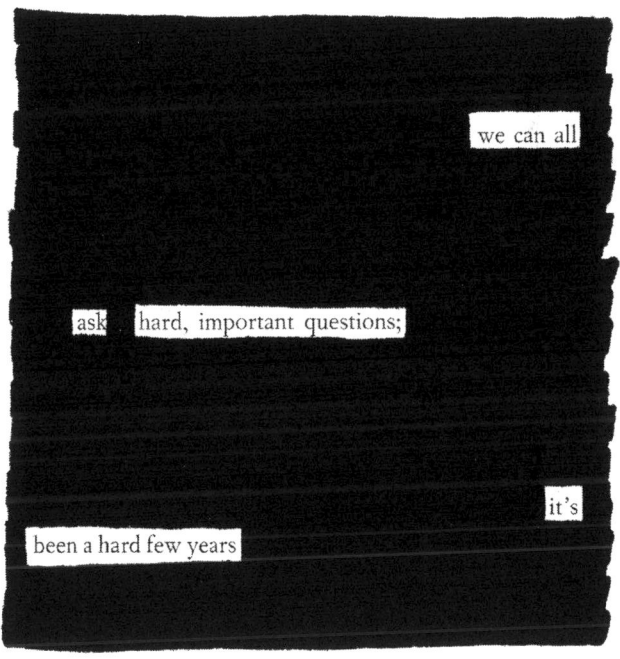

we can all

ask hard, important questions;

it's
been a hard few years

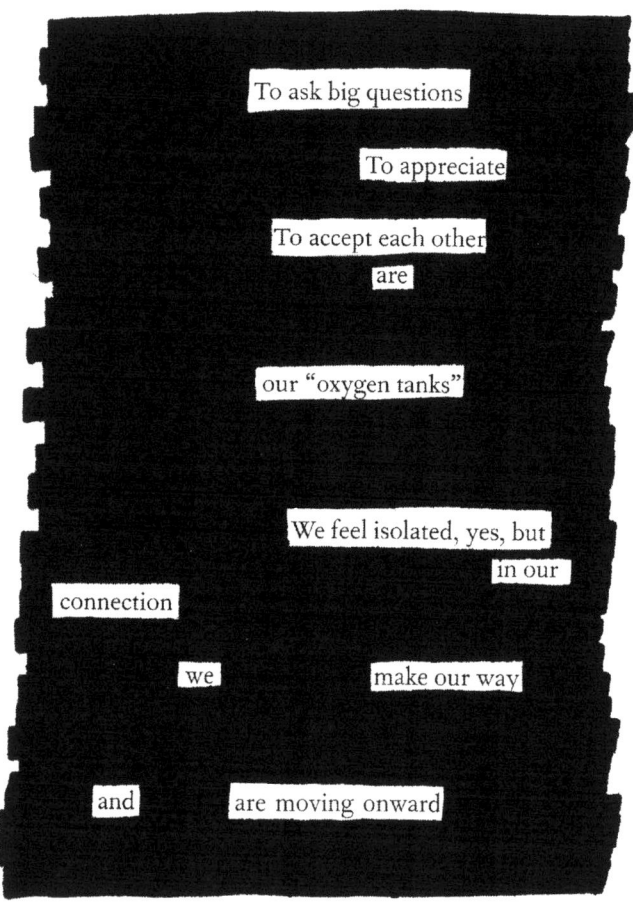

To ask big questions

To appreciate

To accept each other
are

our "oxygen tanks"

We feel isolated, yes, but
in our
connection
we make our way

and are moving onward

Embrace the changing
plan
to calm
the push-pull
struggle
everything now
all together

is
just growing up

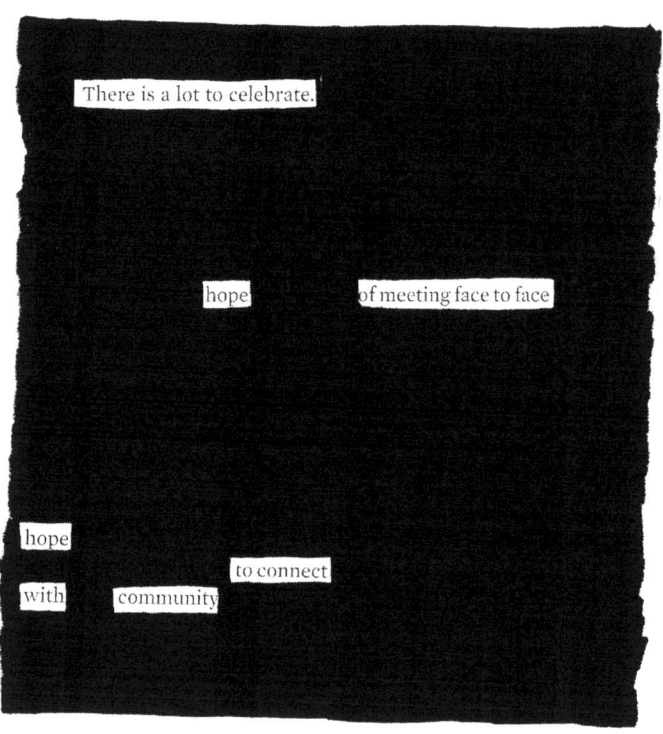

One person can make a difference—
ripple s
of heartfelt gratitude
bond
community together.

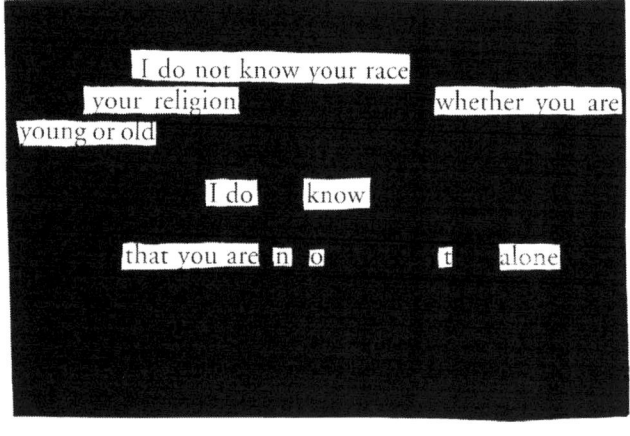

SOURCE TEXTS

64 Parishes, no. 4 (Summer 2019).

Centenary Magazine, Fall 2017.

Centenary Magazine, Fall 2018.

Colette. *The Vagabond*. Translated by Enid McLeod. New   York: Farrar, Straus, and Giroux, 1982.

Collingwood, R. G. *The Principles of Art*. New York: Oxford University Press, 1958.

Corrigan, Kelly. *Tell Me More: Stories about the 12 Hardest Things I'm Learning to Say*. New York: Random House, 2018.

Golf Digest, no. 9 (2020).

Henslin, James M. *Essentials of Sociology: A Down-to-Earth Approach*, 7th ed. Boston: Pearson, 2007.

Mursell, Gordon, ed. *The Story of Christian Spirituality: Two Thousand Years, from East to West*. Oxford: Fortress Press, 2001.

New York Times, September 18, 2020.

New York Times, November 11, 2020.

Psychotherapy Networker Magazine, September/October 2018.

Psychotherapy Networker Magazine, September/October 2020.

Runner's World, no. 1 (2019).

Scientific American, May 2019.

Shreveport Magazine, Fall 2017.

Shreveport Magazine, Fall 2018.

ACKNOWLEDGEMENTS

No book is made alone, and I must voice my gratitude in closing:

To Austin Kleon, for introducing me to blackout poetry from afar, and to the creators of each aforementioned source text—without whom these poems would not exist.

To everyone who has resonated with this work, conversed about it, shared it online, or preordered the book. Your support spurred me on to the finish line. To Brandon Winngingham, for inviting me to teach your Captain Shreve High School students about blackout poetry. To the Meadows Museum of Art at Centenary College, for the opportunity to show a selection of the original poems in your gallery.

To Jennifer Strange, for your kind edits and curiosity. They significantly improved this project and readied it for others.

To my parents, Beth and Rick Duet. Without your limitless love and support, I would not be here to make anything at all.

And to Kirk Reedstrom, my partner in everything. Thank you for believing in me and my work every day. We did this.

HOW TO MAKE BLACKOUT POEMS

SUPPLIES
- Source texts (old newspaper, magazine, book, etc.)
- Pencil with eraser
- Black marker (like a fine point or chisel tip Sharpie)

STEPS
- Choose a source text.
- Skim the page, using a pencil to underline words that interest you.
- Edit! Box in words to form a coherent poem.
- Mark through the remaining words with your black marker and erase any visible pencil lines.

TIPS
- Blackout at least 50% of the page.
- Don't use more than 3 or 4 words in a row.
- Find words within words or combine various letters in a line of text to form new words.
- Say something new. (Don't summarize source text.)
- Credit the source if publishing.

ABOUT THE AUTHOR

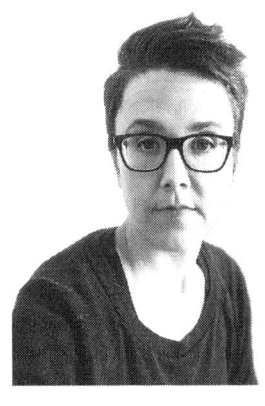

SARAH DUET (she/her) is an interdisciplinary artist and writer. The exploration of who we are, how we're connected, and why it matters persists in her work across mediums. Often combining visual and literary elements, she invites viewers into quiet reflection and personal discovery through layers of meaning, texture, and minimal palettes. She lives with her husband, Kirk Reedstrom, and their quirky cat, Nash, in Shreveport, LA.

Sarah's art and writing have been published in *Point of Vue Magazine*, *Art House America*, *Heliopolis*, *Pandora Art and Literary Magazine*, and *Enneagram Magazine*. This collection, *What Happened is Happening: Poems,* is her first book of blackout poetry.

You can subscribe to her newsletter, **MAKE THINGS & SHARE THEM**, and follow her work at **sarahduet.com**.